CATS ^and dogs^ ARE PEOPLE TOO!

Painting by the author.

C ATS *and dogs* ARE P EOPLE T OO *!*

*A Look into the Vile and
Insensitive Attitudes that
Result in Commercial Pet Food
with Health-Promoting Alternatives
that are Easy to Incorporate into Your Lifestyle.*

S HARON G ANNON

J IVAMUKTI P RESS N EW Y ORK C ITY

JIVAMUKTI PRESS
404 Lafayette Street
New York, NY 10003

877-I AM YOGA
http://www.jivamuktiyoga.com

Book Design by Barbara Boris
Production Assistance by Gail Berrigan

Cover photo of Sharon and Thai Tea
sharing corn on the cob.

Reprinted from DR. PITCAIRN'S COMPLETE GUIDE
TO NATURAL HEALTH FOR DOGS & CATS ©1995 by
Richard H. Pitcairn & Susan H. Pitcairn. Permission granted by Rodale
Press, Inc; Emmaus, PA 18098. Available wherever books are sold or
directly from the publisher by calling
(800) 848-4735 or visit our website at www.rodalestore.com

"The Far Reach of the Barbaric Fur Trade: Asia's
Dog and Cat Fur Business," *The Animals' Agenda*,
Vol. 19, No.1, pp.40-41. Reprinted with permission from The
Animals' Agenda, PO Box 25881, Baltimore, MD 21224; (410) 675-
4566; www.animalsagenda.org

"The Dark Side of Rendering" appearing in the *Nexus Magazine* and
originally in *Earth Island Journal*. Reprinting permission kindly
granted by Nexus Magazine, PO Box 30, Mapleton Qld, 4560
Australia; www.peg.apc.org/-nexus and Earth Island Journal, 300
Broadway, #28, San Francisco, CA 94133 (415) 788-3666;
www.earthisland.org

Printed in the United States of America.
Library of Congress Catalog Card Number: 99-95492
ISBN 0-9655-884-6-7

A portion of the proceeds from the sale of this book
will go to benefit PETA and the Animal Mukti program
of the Humane Society of New York.

There is a saying in Sanskrit:

लोकः समस्थ सुखीनोः भवन्तु

Lokah Samasta Sukhinoh Bhavantu
May all beings, everywhere, be happy and free.

This book is dedicated
to the loving and patient cats
who have felt that I was worthwhile
enough to spend a lifetime with.
Especially: Patience, Taffy, Little Eva,
Gezar of Ling, Kit Kat and Mr. Mouse.

Acknowledgments

SPECIAL THANKS TO:
David Life for his editing skills, encouragement and support of this project, but most importantly for his shameless and boundless love of cats, dogs and me. Jenny Meyer for her editing skills without which this book would be unreadable. Barbara Boris for the design and construction of this book. But more important, thank you Barbara for the generous hospitality you have always shown to me and my cats in spite of your allergies. We love you very much.

Sandra DeFeo for her unwavering optimism and tireless work to make this world a better place for cats, dogs and people. It is encouraging to know that a vegetarian who practices meditation is the director of the Humane Society of New York. Eleanor Molbegott for her patience, attention to detail and legal expertise. Robin Bowman for her enchanting photographs of Thai Tea and Mamuska at home, and the appreciation she shows to all the cats and dogs she meets. Janet Rienstra for her support and reading of the early manuscript and for giving me valuable criticism as well as continuous encouragement. Mike D. and Tamra Davis for the love and compassion they show to all sentient beings and for their courage to take social action in the name of peace and animal rights. Rufus and Louie for trying out my recipes and giving commentary. V.V. Tobier for being my friend and a loving and generous friend to cats. Uma for being ever present.

Trudie Styler and Sting for making their home a model home, a sanctuary where dogs and cats are treated as family members. Russell Simmons for encouraging me to be a fearless voice for those who can't speak up for themselves. Kristin Leigh and Amy Santos for happily assisting me in my daily work. Ann N. Martin for graciously giving me permission to use excerpts from her courageous book, "*Food Pets Die For*," and for encouraging me to write this book.

My beloved Gurus, Shri Brahmananda Sarasvati, Shri Swami Nirmalananda and Shri K. Pattabhi Jois for giving me the grace to teach Yoga as a spiritual practice.

Thai Tea, Mamuska, Ursula and Miten for loving me as their special person and teaching me that cats are people too!

S.G.
New York City
July 1999

Table of Contents

Preface by Sandra DeFeo 13

Introduction 15

1. Are You Feeding Dead Cats and Dogs to Your Pets? 21

2. What to do Next: The 9 Step Program
   for Happy Cats Through Healthy Meals 31

3. Vegetables, Grains and Beans 34

4. Important Nutritional Supplements 40

5. Should a Vegetarian Serve Meat
   to Their Cat and Dog Friends? 47

6. Sample Meals 53

   Casserole Convenience Meals..59

7. Poisonous Plants, Flowers and Cleaning Products 65

8. The Way to a Cat's Heart is
   Not Always Through the Stomach 67

   Cleanliness 67

   Cutting Nails...67

   Litter Box..70

   Climbing 71

   Fresh Air Outings 72

   Bathing 74

   Allergies...74

   Fleas...75

   Noise Pollution 76

   Lone Cats 76

   Spaying and Neutering 77

9. Trust 78

10. Yoga Teachings on Non-Violence 81

11. Teachings of Love and Kindness from Dog People 82

12. Education 87

Afterward 91

AUTHOR'S NOTE:
I am an animal lover, not a scientist or doctor. Information in this book is based solely on my experience and on my relationship to my own companion animals. Readers are urged to consult a veterinarian before making any changes to their pets' diet or lifestyle.

Preface

In *"Cats are People Too,"* Sharon Gannon takes us on a journey to a higher consciousness and many valuable lessons are learned along the way. Starting with the physical she asks us to rethink our pet's nutrition. Many people do not even consider their own nutrition. It takes a short walk through any supermarket to see that much of the food consumed by our fellow human beings is not all it can be. Sharon gently reprimands us by confronting us with truths she has searched for and found, challenging us to meet our pet's nutritional needs with more care and consideration.

Although what our pets eat is a very important focus of this book, there is so much more. Sharon makes us think like a cat and understand a dog's heightened sense of smell. Our senses are intensified and our mind expands as we follow her path. We start with a diet and wind up contemplating the habitat. The whole environment: Physical, Emotional and Spiritual.

Cats and dogs satisfy the human species' need for companionship and unconditional love. They teach us so many things. Serving them is our honor and our joy. Sharon re-invigorates our appreciation of our loyal pals. We come to a much deeper understanding of their natural, crucial place in our universe: from sleeping at the end of the bed to their igniting of our better, more compassionate selves.

Sharon, thank you for asking us to open our eyes to see what you have seen about our animal friends and ultimately what we need to see about ourselves.

Sandra DeFeo
Co-Executive Director
Humane Society of New York

Introduction

I have always loved animals. Since childhood I have felt very uneasy in situations where cruelty or humiliation occurred toward any creature. It is mainly to cats that I have felt a connection— a companionship equal to the humans I have known. Ridiculed for my love and defense of animals, I quickly learned as a child that we live in a human-centered world, where animals are not deemed worthy of the same considerations we take for granted as human beings. Does the way we treat animals have an effect on the way in which we treat other human beings and ourselves? Does the quality of our relationships with other beings have a bearing on our own happiness? These questions intrigued me as a child and still do.

SEATTLE PERFORMER

During the 1970s I lived in Seattle, Washington, and worked as a stage performer, an actress, a dancer and a musician. I did not see a huge division between art, spirituality and social action.

Jesse Bernstein, a local playwright, wrote a play called *The Dead Dog*, in which I had a leading part. During rehearsals Jesse told us that he wanted to have an actual dead dog placed downstage during the entirety of the performance. I immediately objected for ethical reasons and asked him where he intended to find one. He replied in a very matter of fact way, "From the rendering plant. You can come with me, if you want. We'll buy a dog before it's sold to the pet food factory; it'll be cheap!" Jesse said he used to work at the local rendering plant in Seattle. "Where do you think all those animals that are put to sleep at the pound go?" he asked. I wanted to see for myself. The truth can be horrifying but it can also inspire you to action. As the great animal rights/human rights activist Henry Spira said, "When you see something that's wrong, you've got to do something about it."

The outcome of my eye opener was that we didn't use an actual dog, instead we had a stage prop made. But I wrote a song about it called *"Are You Feeding Dog Meat to Your Dog?"* and sang it with my band. I honestly don't think that our audience took what I said seriously, after all it was merely art. Just lyrics in a song.

My growing discontent with the role of artist in our culture gradually led me to put more and more energy into attempting to get to the heart of the matter. I wrote political and metaphysical essays and hosted a weekly study group called the Salon Apocalypse where issues such as animal rights, vegetarianism, mysticism and Eastern and Western philosophies could be discussed. I continued to perform but felt a growing separation between stage and audience, or rather between art and life.

During this time I saw a documentary that changed my life and gave me renewed courage. The film was *"The Animals Film,"* narrated by Julie Christie with music by Robert Wyatt. Prior to my exposure to the film, I was an on-again, off-again vegetarian. After seeing it I became a committed vegan and wanted to do something to stop the insanity of speciesism.

TEACHING YOGA IN NEW YORK CITY

I moved to New York City in the early '80s and began to seriously pursue the study of Yoga and meditation. I started to teach simple Yogic techniques as part of my performances. The Salon continued in New York City and I brought Yogic teachings into these gatherings as well. The practices of Yoga deal with training your perception to see deeply into things, to perceive root causes rather than symptoms. Yoga states that the purpose of life is to know eternal happiness and that happiness is the source of all creation. In truth we are one with this source. To know yourself as one with this source you begin by practicing to see yourself in others. As long as you perceive others as different from you, you do not perceive the One. The first step in this development of clear perception is called *ahimsa*. It is the first step on the Yogic path. It means non-harming. The Yoga teachings tell us that until you see only One, treat who and what you see with kindness and compassion. Yoga is a practical philosophy, which says that to know something you must have an experience; an intellectual or emotional connection is not enough. Through my work in the arts I was only connecting intellectually and emotionally to my audience. I wanted to give something more. I wanted to give the tools with which people could have an elevated experience.

When I began teaching Yoga full time, I included vegetarianism and animal rights in my curriculum. My classes continue to be centered around the practice of *asana*. To most people this usually means the classical physical postures without any philosophical foundation. As a teacher, I cannot exclude the spiritual, psychological and philosophical teachings from the physical aspects of Yoga. The Sanskrit word asana means seat, and seat means a connection to the earth. In this sense earth refers to things as well as beings. So the practice of Yoga asana really means the practice of perfecting our connection to the earth through perfecting our relationships with all things and beings. The term 'all beings' includes human as well as non-human animals. The first place to concentrate on creating a more peaceful world is in your immediate sphere: your home, your family, and the animals that live with you.

I developed relationships with the many people who came to me for Yogic instruction. People who wanted to improve themselves, to evolve, to break free of debilitating habits and addictions. I loved and admired the ambitions in the hearts of these Yogi wannabees. But it did not occur to many of these people that their own desire for a natural and healthy lifestyle that is spiritually inspiring should reflect on the quality of life they were providing for their companion animals. I visited many of these people and was saddened to see a single cat in residence with no other creatures of its kind to keep it company. These cats were living in small cramped New York City apartments for their whole lives, never touching paws to earth, deprived of fresh air and direct sunlight. Although my students were eating macrobiotic health food their cats and dogs were eating highly processed commercial pet food. In 1989 I decided to give a workshop entitled "How To Brighten Your Cat's Life."

The workshop was very well received. I presented material through a slide show which showed my cats eating 'human' type food containing lots of vegetables, going for outings on leashes to the park, climbing on tree branches which I had installed in my cat-friendly apartment. I talked about the rendered ingredients that went into some commercial pet food, which include euthanized cats and dogs.

At the end of the lecture and slideshow all the participants were given a shopping bag filled with items for them and their cats. They were given cans of salmon, tuna and sardines, fresh raw hamburger, turkey and chicken, clover sprouts, nutritional yeast and lecithin, an assortment of organic produce and grains (as well as canned and dry *Wysong* brand natural pet food). Along with this goodie bag they were given typed-out instructions on how to begin incorporating this new type of food into their cats' diet. They were also given instructions on how to build an outdoor enclosed area which could fit securely on the side of a New York City building. This would enable their cat to receive the benefits of fresh air and sunshine without the hazards of the street. I emphasized the need to drop the common prejudices that relegate cats to an inferior position and to begin to see cats and other non-human animals as people too.

A CATS-TORICAL LOOK

Opening a can or a box and slapping the contents in a bowl does not fulfill our obligation to our companion animal. I investigated this habit. Where did it begin?

In ancient Egypt cats were worshipped. They were also loved as family members. In the typical Egyptian home all family members shaved their eyebrows in mourning when the family cat died. From this exalted height the status of the cat plummeted. In Europe, between the thirteenth and eighteenth centuries cats were perceived as being the familiars of witches. They were abused and tortured accordingly. By the Victorian era cats were no longer feared as demons but they were still far from the cherished, coddled companions of today. Tolerated for their rodent catching abilities, they were compelled to catch their own dinner, or starve. This attitude changed dramatically when the British illustrator Louis Wain fell in love with a rain soaked black and white orphaned kitten named Peter.

LOUIS WAIN
AN ARTIST WHO CHANGED OUR ATTITUDE TOWARDS CATS

I have always admired the work of Louis Wain, the Victorian cat artist. He saw and painted cats as people. Wain shifted our perceptions about cats at a time in history when the relationship between cats and humans was in dire need of change.

This nineteenth century artist charmed the British public with his humorous illustrations of cats wearing spectacles, riding bicycles, shopping and dressing for the opera. Suddenly humans could see themselves in cats.

It all began with Peter the homeless kitten. One rainy night Wain's wife, bedridden with a fatal disease, heard a little kitten crying at her window. Wain's initial response, like any Londoner of the day was, *"Scat Cat!"* But his wife was adamant, and over Wain's protestations the wet kitten was brought in. Peter quickly became a member of the family for this childless couple. The more time Wain spent with little Peter the more in love with the kitten he became until he truly saw him as his child. Louis Wain's biographer, Heather Latimer, describes Wain and Peter sharing buttered toast, a soft-boiled egg and tea together each morning.

By now the artist had taken to sketching the kitten in his leisure time. The charming form of the cat quickly overtook his artistic imagination and soon all of his illustrations were of cat-people. His work became so popular that he could not keep up with the demand and soon other artists began to copy him. The rage of the 1880s was cat-people postcards. Louis Wain brought into vogue the term *Catland*, a state of mind where people begin to see others with whiskers, tails, paws and fur. Wain's artistic vision effected the way that people viewed cats. Instead of only being seen as mice and rat controllers they were given a new status as people too!

Unfortunately there was a downside to this shift in consciousness. As time went on, and humans and felines became inseparable, enterprising businessmen did not fail to see a good opportunity. *Voila! Cat Food.* The age of commercial pet food was born.

1

Are You Feeding Dead Cats and Dogs to Your Pets?

*"I care not for a man's religion
whose dogs and cats are not the better for it."*

ABRAHAM LINCOLN

Years after mad cow disease was linked to the cannibalistic feeding of cows to cows, rendered animals are still routinely used in some pet food and commercial feed. We are feeding our cows, pigs, chickens, dogs and cats to their own kind. Those of us who consume meat and dairy products are, however inadvertently, eating the recycled remains of these animals. Mad cow disease is not the only threat we face. As Gar Smith reported in *Nexus Magazine* and *Earth Island Journal,*

> *Transmissable spongiform encephalopathy (TSE) carried in pig- and chicken-laden foods may eventually eclipse the threat of "mad cow disease."*
>
> *The risk of household pet exposure to TSE from contaminated pet food is more than three times greater than the risk for hamburger-eating humans.*

THIS BOOK WILL INSPIRE YOU TO:

1. *Take a closer look at what your companion animal is eating.*

2. *Deepen your own research and investigations of the subjects presented in this book.* See CHAPTER 12 on EDUCATION to supplement the information in this book. Knowledge and awareness are powerful tools.

3. *Be of service to the higher consciousness which allows us to perceive all life as worthy of respect.* Promote the blossoming of love and compassion and allow that to spread to all. The best way to improve our own lives is to do what we can to improve the lives of others. As our pet's diet and lifestyle is improved so is our own.

In her groundbreaking book, "*Food Pets Die For*," Ann Martin writes, "Pets in pet food? No, you say? Be assured that this is happening. Rendered companion animals are just another source of protein used in both pet food and livestock feed."

Aside from possibly containing other cats and dogs, some commercial pet foods may also contain diseased, condemned or contaminated animals. Waste products of the slaughter house which can't pass the government's standards for human grade food are permitted. Some materials that may be used in the formulas are by no stretch of the imagination edible food. Items like sawdust, feces, pesticides, fur and heavy metals (from cattle and dog ID tags as well as metal bands from the legs of chickens). The fur is not removed from euthanized animals; many still wearing their flea collars are shoved in the rendering pit, often wrapped in their plastic body bags.

Let us wake up! Let us not be duped by advertising! No longer will we walk into a grocery store, and like an automaton, pull a box off the shelf because it is labeled 'cat food' or 'dog food,' and then go home and sprinkle these kibbles into a bowl and think we have done a good job of feeding our animal friend! You certainly wouldn't expect any level of good health for yourself if you limited the food you ate day in and day out for your entire lifetime to some highly processed, condemned-for-human consumption material coming from a box, bag or can. How can we think our cat or dog would not suffer ill consequences due to such a diet? We should never rely totally on processed, commercially available pet food: canned, dry, moist, boxed, bagged or whatever.

The most frequently asked question in my practice is, "Which commercial pet food do you recommend?" My standard answer is "None." I am certain that pet owners notice changes in their animals after using different batches of the same brand of pet food. Their pets may have diarrhea, increased flatulence, a dull hair coat, intermittent vomiting or prolonged scratching. These are symptoms associated with commercial pet foods.

NEXUS MAGAZINE and EARTH ISLAND JOURNAL, Dr. Wendell O. Belfield, D.V.M

Every year the American public gives more than 11 billion dollars to these multi-billion dollar corporations. Slick advertising assures us that the meat, grains, and fats used in these products are of the highest quality and could even grace our own dining tables. *Then why is it being sold as pet food?* I don't feed my cats this stuff. When the truth is known I am sure no intelligent, caring human being could continue to degrade their loving, loyal companion animal by feeding them this kind of 'food.'

> *Recycling dead pets and wildlife into animal food is a "very small part of the business that we don't like to advertise." Valley Proteins President J.J. Smith told the [Baltimore] Sun Paper. The plant processes these animals as a "public service, not for profit," Smith said, since "there is not a lot of protein and fat on pets.... just a lot of hair you have to deal with somehow."*
>
> NEXUS MAGAZINE and EARTH ISLAND JOURNAL, Gar Smith

According to the U.S. Department of Agriculture there is no mandatory inspection of pet food ingredients. Our government needs to do more to hold the pet food manufacturers accountable for the ingredients in their products. The attitude seems to be one of anything goes. After all it's just pet food. Something for an 'animal.'

ARE WE PROMOTING CANNIBALISM?

Are *your* cats and dogs eating other cats and dogs? Every month millions of dogs and cats are euthanized by city animal shelters and veterinarians throughout the country. Where do these bodies end up? The minority are given a respectable burial or cremation. According to the *New York Times*, most of these unwanted bodies are picked up by various sanitation companies and rendered. The rendered material is then sold to some pet food companies. Ann Martin writes,

> *When I began investigating the ingredients used in commercial pet food, a veterinarian in the United States advised me that the*

*use of pets in pet food was routine practice. Rendering is a cheap
viable means of disposal for euthanized pets.*

It was no surprise to me to find out that some of the executives
appointed to run the Center for Animal Care and Control (CACC)
in New York City have little experience in animal welfare and
well-being. Their backgrounds are in waste management. John
Doherty, chairman of the CACC in 1999 is also the Sanitation
Commissioner. The recently appointed director of the CACC,
Marilyn Haggerty-Blohm came from the Mayor's office where she
primarily dealt with solid waste management.

According to *New York Magazine* the city euthanizes over 40,000
animals every year in their Animal Shelter programs.

> *There are plenty of things this city does right. Taking care of
> its lost or unwanted pets isn't one of them. Given the number of
> New Yorkers who care about cats and dogs, do we really have to
> kill 40,000 of them every year?*
>
> *New Yorkers are taxed just 75 cents a year for animal
> control—a little more than half the national average.*

SHELTER SKELTER, Elizabeth Hess, NEW YORK MAGAZINE, 10/19/98

On the other hand, how much money does the average New
Yorker spend on 'dog food' and 'cat food' each year?

It doesn't take a genius to put two and two together. There
must be an underlying reason for the deplorable way that New
York City treats its homeless pet population. Money is being made
somewhere down the line. The Mayor assures us the problem is
being handled. By appointing people whose experience is in
waste management and garbage disposal to executive positions in
charge of the destiny of unwanted cats and dogs, New York *is*
solving the problem. Our city government needs incentives to
reduce the number of animals killed every year.

In *"Food Pets Die For,"* Ann Martin quotes a 1997 *New York Times*
article:

> *Renderers in the United States pick up one hundred million
> pounds of waste material every day—a witches brew of feet,
> heads, stomachs, intestines, hooves, spinal cords, tails, grease,*

A cat awaiting adoption.

feathers and bones.... An estimated six million to seven million
dogs and cats are killed in animal shelters each year, said Jeff
Frace, a spokesman for the American Society for the Prevention
of Cruelty to Animals.
   For example, the city of Los Angeles sends two hundred
tons of euthanized dogs and cats to West Coast Rendering,
in Los Angeles, every month, according to Chuck Ellis, a
spokesperson for the city's sanitation department.

In February 1990, *The San Francisco Chronicle* published a
chilling story about stray dogs and cats who are collected from
pounds and (sometimes unwitting) veterinarians. These animals
are then sent to rendering plants where they are ground up
into pet food. Reporter John Eckhouse described how pet food
companies deny this is happening, yet a rendering industry
employee confided that it was "common practice for his company
to process pets into products sold to pet food manufacturers."

   The rendering plant floor is piled high with 'raw product':
   thousands of dead dogs and cats; heads and hooves from cattle,
   sheep, pigs and horses; whole skunks; rats and raccoons all
   waiting to be processed. In the 90-degree heat, the piles of dead

animals seem to have a life of their own as millions of maggots swarm over the carcasses.

Two bandanna-masked men begin operating Bobcat mini-dozers, loading the "raw" into a 10-foot-deep stainless-steel pit. They are undocumented workers from Mexico, doing a dirty job. A giant auger-grinder at the bottom of the pit begins to turn. Popping bones and squeezing flesh are sounds from a nightmare you will never forget.

Rendering is the process of cooking raw animal material to remove the moisture and fat. The rendering plant works like a giant kitchen.... Once the mass is cut into small pieces, it is transported to another auger for fine shredding. It is then cooked at 280 degrees for one hour. This continuous batch cooking process goes on non-stop, 24 hours a day, seven days a week as meat is melted away from bones in hot 'soup.' During this cooking process, the 'soup' produces a fat of yellow grease or tallow that rises to the top and is skimmed off. [To be used in the making of candles, soap and cosmetics.] The cooked meat and bone are sent to a hammermill press, which squeezes out the remaining moisture and pulverizes the product into a gritty powder.... Once the batch is finished, all that is left is yellow grease, meat and bone meal.

As the American Journal of Veterinary Research explains, this recycled meat and bone meal is used "as a source of protein and other nutrients in the diets of poultry and swine and in pet foods with lesser amounts used in the feed of cattle and sheep. Animal fat is also used in animal feeds as an energy source." Everyday, hundreds of rendering plants across the United States truck millions of tons of this "food enhancer" to poultry ranches, cattle feed-lots, dairy and hog farms, fish-feed plants and pet-food manufacturers where it is mixed with other ingredients to feed billions of animals that meat eating humans, in turn, will eat.

NEXUS MAGAZINE, 12/96-1/97 and EARTH ISLAND JOURNAL, Fall 1990

It is not only other cats and dogs we may be feeding to our pets, but animals raised for slaughter that are rejected as 4-D—dead, diseased, dying and disabled. According to Ann Martin, this vile brew could also contain old meat past the 'sale date' from supermarket shelves (including the Styrofoam tray and cellophane wrapping), rancid restaurant grease, roadkill, and some zoo animals.

> *The slaughterhouses where cattle, pigs, goats, calves, sheep, poultry and rabbits meet their fate provide more fuel for rendering. After slaughter, heads, feet, skin, toenails, hair, feathers, carpal and tarsal joints and mammary glands are removed. This material is sent to rendering. Animals that have died on their way to slaughter are rendered. Cancerous tissue or tumors and worm-infested organs are rendered. Injection sites, blood clots, bone splinters, or extraneous matter are rendered. Contaminated blood is rendered. Stomach and bowels are rendered. Contaminated material containing or having been treated with a substance not permitted by, or in any amount in excess of limits prescribed under the Food and Drug Act or the Environmental Protection Act. In other words, if a carcass contains high levels of drugs or pesticides this material is rendered.*
>
> *Before rendering, this material from the slaughterhouse is "denatured," which means that the material from the slaughter-house is covered with a particular substance to prevent it from getting back into the human food chain. In the United States the substances used for denaturing include: crude carbolic acid, fuel oil, or citronella.*

FOOD PETS DIE FOR, Ann N. Martin

NOTE: For a more detailed investigation into pets and pet food, read *"Food Pets Die For,"* by Ann N. Martin, *New Sage Press*, Oregon, 1997.

I also wonder whether some of the bodies of the animals used for animal experiments in the thousands of labs and universities across the country end up as rendered material. Why not? If someone could make money from it they might, perhaps, try.

Many people that I talk to about the ingredients used in pet food are surprised to hear that euthanized pets could possibly be used. But they somehow accept that the by-products of the meat industry, the stuff that can't be sold to humans is acceptable food for pets. Why? I think because we have always given our domesticated dogs and cats the leftovers from the hunt. People are still living with the quaint idea that the 'leftovers' of the factory farm slaughterhouse are the same. They are not.

Feeding our companion animals the remains of their brothers and sisters is not only morally objectionable, it is downright dangerous. Sodium pentobarbital is a drug that is used to euthanize pets. According to a 1993 report of the American Veterinary Medical Association *Panel on Euthanasia,* sodium pentobarbital should not be administered to animals intended for food. This barbiturate survives the high temperatures used in rendering. It remains in the tissues and is then ingested by our companion animals.

ARE ALL COMMERCIAL PET FOODS HARMFUL?

Some are better than others. They certainly should not be the primary source of food for your pet. Be wary of so-called health food products, which offer a 'pet-product' line. Some time ago, I was given a jar of spirulina powder for cats by a well-meaning friend. I did not give it to my cats because when I examined it, it looked like the dregs of the extraction process, and it probably was. I only give my cats spirulina powder which is of a quality to be consumed by people. After all, cats are people too.

As you make the transition from packaged to healthy cat meals, it might be helpful to serve some commercial cat food along with the new food. If you feel you must do this, check the ingredients on the label. Avoid anything which has meat by-products, meat meal, meat, bone meal, poultry meal, poultry by-products, beef by-products, fish meal, fish oil, tallow, beef fat, and chicken fat. Also avoid anything that says 'vegetable protein,' which is little more than the sweepings from the milling room floors.

Eileen Layne of the California Veterinary Medical Association told the *San Francisco Chronicle,* "When you read pet food labels and it says 'meat and bone meal,' that's what it is: cooked and converted animals, including some cats and dogs."

This is all the more reason why we need some government regulations in rendering facilities.

If I were to recommend a brand of canned or packaged pet food it would be *Wysong* brand. This brand is found in most pet food stores that carry 'health-food' type cat and dog foods. Dr. R. L. Wysong never makes arrogant claims that his pet foods are 100% balanced and complete. He suggests that you use his products, which include dry and canned dog and cat food, to supplement a diet of fresh foods including meats, grains and vegetables. He offers a vegan dry food for cats and dogs. Dr. Wysong promotes education and common sense over marketing ploys. All the meats, grains and vegetables in his products are 'human grade.' The website is www.wysong.net, telephone (517) 631-8801.

Pet food manufacturers insist that they know all there is to know about the nutritional requirements of cats and dogs. But much more research has been conducted on the nutritional needs of human beings than of cats and dogs, and still the results are not completely known or agreed upon.

I do not recommend the pre-packaged prescription diet foods that many veterinarians sell. Besides the usual rendered material that may be in these products, they may also contain ethoxyquin, a toxic preservative which is banned by the FDA for human consumption. Ethoxyquin was originally developed as a rubber stabilizer. According to Ann Martin, ethoxyquin is classified as a pesticide that is hazardous when ingested. *The Consumers Dictionary of Food Additives* says that ethoxyquin "has been found to cause liver tumors in new-born mice." The company that markets ethoxyquin has affixed a prominent skull and crossbones to the label reading, Caution/Poison. But the absence of ethoxyquin on the pet food label does not mean your pet is safe. Pet food manufacturers are not required to list the substance if it was added at the rendering facility, only if they added it themselves.

How many parents would take the advice of a pediatrician who placed a packaged food product on the exam table and told the parent that this is the only thing they should feed their child day in, day out, for the child's lifetime, and further that they should be sure not to feed any other foods because they might unbalance the product?

This is a dangerous mindset that permeates the pet food industry, nutritionists, health professionals and government officials who say that only processed, toxic and contaminated food is the best food for pets.

RATIONALE FOR ANIMAL NUTRITION, Dr. R.L. Wysong

2

What to do Next:
The 9 Step Program for Happy Cats
Through Healthy Meals

1. Cats and dogs are to be considered as family members.
They should be shown respect and treated in such a way that they
enjoy the highest quality of experiences that life with you can
afford. Just as you would visit a doctor for your regular checkups,
so should your pet. A veterinarian can determine if the nutritional
needs of your companion animals are being met.

**2. Cats and dogs are not lesser animals with inferior
likes and needs than humans.** Most humans accept the idea
that animals are inferior. This belief is used to justify feeding sub-
standard food to pets. This belief also leads to depriving cats of
fresh air, fresh water and sunlight. Speciesism is so subtly
ingrained in our minds that it goes unnoticed and unquestioned.
Until very recently racism and sexism were condoned in our
culture. Now it is time to put a halt to speciesism.

**3. Don't feed your cat and dogs anything that has not been
approved for human consumption.** That's a beginning. Once you
can accept that, you can be more discriminating about acceptable
foods. In other words, resist advertising propaganda which
exhorts you to buy dry or canned or semi-moist pet food. Even
supplements or vitamins that are marketed for pets should be
questioned and usually avoided.

4. Never leave food available for nibbling throughout the day.
Pick up bowls after 30-45 minutes and wash them. The mere smell
of food triggers the cat's brain to release chemicals that turn the
urine alkaline. This is desirable when the cat is actually eating. But

a constant alkaline level can lead to urinary infections and feline urologic syndrome (FUS). Allowing cats to nibble throughout the day will also suppress their immune system. Allow them to develop a healthy appetite. Do not keep them in a state of dullness by inhibiting the normal digestive enzymes which will be triggered by an empty stomach and the attractive smell of a fresh meal. An exception would be an elderly cat who may require several small meals throughout the day. As cats (and humans) age they are less proficient at digesting nutrients.

5. Serve each meal in a clean bowl that has been washed well in hot soapy water. Be sure to rinse well so no detergent residue remains. Cats have very sensitive noses and will be able to detect the smallest amount of detergent residue. It is best to use a non-toxic soap, one that is also ecologically friendly.

6. Use glass, china or stainless steel bowls; never use plastic. Plastic can release gases, creating unpleasant smells. It can also cause chin acne. Little nicks and abrasions can develop in plastic which can harbor germs and bacteria. Some ceramic bowls have lead-based glazes, which make them very toxic to cats, dogs and humans. Check and find out if the bowl is lead-free. If this information isn't available to you don't take a chance; use something else. Also, cats like low sides on their bowls so their whiskers don't touch.

7. Always supply clean filtered or bottled water in a clean bowl everyday. Never allow tap water to be the only source of water for your animal friend. Chlorine destroys vitamin E in the body. Most water coming from city water taps is recycled sewer water that has been disinfected with chlorine.

Once out of the tap, chlorine evaporates; unfortunately, chlorine combines with any organic substances which may be in the water to form chloroform, a poisonous cancer-causing chemical which does not evaporate.

HEALING WITH WHOLE FOODS, Paul Pitchford

8. *Never feed the same food day in and day out.* Variety
should be the theme in preparing meals for your animal friends.
They go through cycles of likes and dislikes; they may not feel
like eating something that they seemed to love eating last week.
Like people, cats and dogs can be flexible or stubborn, and
every shade in between. A variety of foods provides a safer way
to ensure that they don't become deficient in a particular area
of nutrition. Feeding the same food over and over, even if it is
good health-giving food, can induce food allergies as well as
nutritional deficiencies.

**9. *Feed a variety of foods from both plant and animal
sources.*** All food should be organic and of the highest quality.
Fresh is preferred over frozen, dried, or canned. Remember cats
and dogs who have been eating cooked, processed and commercial pet foods have suppressed the normal digestive enzymes in
their systems. It is difficult for them to start eating live foods
or even to properly extract the nutrients from any food they are
eating. Usually they will not have any appetite for live or fresh
foods. Have patience and feel some empathy. Imagine a human
being who has been eating crackers and processed cheese all
of their life. If offered a salad of sprouts, arugula and spirulina,
they probably wouldn't be likely to grab a fork (or chopstick) and
dig in!

3
Vegetables, Grains and Beans

It is very important that you supply fresh raw vegetables to cats that are confined indoors in a house or an apartment. Living beings all need sun. Chlorophyll in green plants is like concentrated sun power. When cats are allowed out of doors they will always nibble on leaves and grasses. It is cruel to deprive cats of these necessary health-inducing food sources.

Fresh foods stimulate the immune system and keep the digestive enzymes active. Eating raw and cooked vegetables keeps the urinary tract healthy and guards against the cat's number one enemy: urinary track diseases such as FUS. This disease can be fatal. In my experience a change from canned or dry cat food has proven to reduce the incidence of FUS. Please add fresh, raw and cooked vegetables to your pet's diet daily.

Make appetizing salads from the following raw vegetables, tossing with flaxseed or olive oil and adding a sprinkle of Kitty Supplement. (See CHAPTER 4 on **IMPORTANT NUTRITIONAL SUPPLEMENTS** for recipe.)

SPROUTS
My cats love all kinds of sprouts, especially clover and radish. They don't care too much for alfalfa but I know of many cats who do. I feed sprouts often, sometimes five times a week.

LETTUCE
Cats seem to love all kinds of lettuce. Organic is always best. Make a salad by cutting or breaking into small pieces.

Retired mouser, currently
employed as lawn mower.

Wild Salad Greens

Sometimes called mesclun salad. My cats love this, the 'wilder' the
better. Try about 2 tablespoons (2 or 3 leaves).

Arugula

This is somewhat bitter, but they love it, it's a real favorite.

Wheat Grass

I buy this already grown at the health food store because when I
tried to grow it for the cats they always ate it before it had a
chance to grow. Wheat grass is a general tonic, immune booster
and blood builder. Sometimes they eat so much it causes them to
throw up a hairball. I feel this is all right; they are using it as a
purgative when they need it.

GRATED CARROT

My cats have always been interested in raw, finely grated carrot. They love it, especially sprinkled with Kitty Supplement. Another favorite sprinkle is parmesan cheese, or soy substitute parmesan cheese.

PARSLEY

Chop it very fine. A good internal cleanser, it helps to promote urine flow, benefiting kidneys and bladder. Parsley can help to remove gravel and soothe an irritated urinary tract. One teaspoon is enough, sprinkled with Kitty Supplement. Or make a tea, serve at room temperature with powdered garlic and a dash of tamari. I add finely chopped parsley to many of my Casserole Convenience Meals. (See CHAPTER 6 on **SAMPLE MEALS** for recipes.)

COOKED VEGETABLES

Be careful not to overcook vegetables. They should still be firm and of bright color. These are some that my cats like: Brussels sprouts, broccoli, cauliflower, green beans, corn, asparagus, summer and winter varieties of squash, yams, sweet potatoes. Red, white or yellow potatoes, kale, beet greens, Swiss chard, peas, lima beans, carrots and garlic.

Vegetables, both raw and cooked, supply much needed fiber to keep the metabolism from getting sluggish. Even meat that is 'fit for human consumption' contains toxins. Feeding your cats vegetables and grains helps them to process the meat better. Vegetables contain necessary minerals and vitamins, and also help to regulate the acid-alkaline balance, guarding against urinary track infections. Vegetables give strength to the nerves, helping a cat deal with stress.

My usual way to cook vegetables is to steam them. Fresh organic vegetables are the best and should make up most of the vegetable choices you offer your cat. Frozen organic vegetables can serve a useful purpose. I keep several packages of frozen peas, corn and lima beans on hand. I rarely if ever give canned vegetables, except beans, as they are too mushy and overcooked and the cats won't eat them.

A sprinkle of Kitty Supplement is great on any of these vegetables. Also try a sprinkle of grated parmesan cheese or soy parmesan. Be versatile, try a sprinkle of chlorella granules or spirulina powder.

SEA VEGETABLES

Sea vegetables, also known as seaweed, are a great source of minerals, vitamins, antioxidants and iodine. Eating seaweed aids digestion, especially in the assimilation of fats, resulting in healthy skin and hair. Seaweed is a medicinal food; it can help detoxify the system from poisons found in food and the environment. Some varieties of sea vegetables that pets like to eat are: dulse, kombu, wakame, kelp, hijiki and arame.

SOME HEALING PROPERTIES OF SEAWEED:

- High in iodine which helps in regulating thyroid function.
- Rich in manganese which activates digestive enzymes.
- Excellent source of calcium, iron and B vitamins.
- Helps to soften hardened tissue areas and tumors.
- Regular consumption (several times a week) will prevent fur and hair loss, and will promote the growth of shiny fur.

Sea vegetables are easy to cook. Boiling or steaming is the best. But you don't have to cook them, just let them soak in boiled water—the longer they soak the more digestible they are. I always have some on hand in the refrigerator, soaking in water. They make a great side dish mixed with other vegetables. Some suggestions you may try are hijiki boiled with lima beans; kombu boiled with potatoes and garlic; hijiki pre-cooked and mixed with grated raw carrots; seaweed mixed with grains like rice, millet or quinoa. Be creative. The point is: cats like vegetables, land and sea alike, cooked and raw. I serve sea vegetables four or five times per week.

Thai Tea always helps to put the groceries away.

GRAINS

Most grains that we humans like to eat, cats also like. In this category I also include bread, pasta, wheat germ and cereal. Please make an effort to only serve organic grains, bread and pasta.

Some of the grains I serve regularly are brown rice, millet, buckwheat (kasha), quinoa, oats, barley and couscous.

Whole wheat bread, toasted or not, buttered and cut into small pieces, makes a great addition to a meal. My cats also like bread soaked in soup broth, or milk or cream (organic, of course).

All shapes of pasta are well-liked, served with butter or oil, and garlic. Sprinkle with Kitty Supplement or chlorella granules or try a sprinkle of parmesan cheese (soy or dairy).

Cooked oatmeal with butter and cream or milk is well liked. My cats' favorite cereal is a dry variety called *Uncle Sam's Cereal*. It is a whole wheat flake with flaxseeds. They love to eat this dry (without milk), as an after dinner snack. For variety mix some toasted wheat germ with the *Uncle Sam's Cereal*, or add a dab of plain yogurt.

BEANS

I keep several cans of beans on hand: aduki, white, navy, lentils and garbanzos. My cats like all of these varieties, but garbanzos are their favorites. I also feed them dried beans which have been cooked in soup. Generally soy beans and soy products are not cat favorites, but I do know cats who like tofu and tempeh.

Only feed a small amount of beans. It is best to feed some grain and seaweed at the same time as this makes the beans easier to digest and less gas-forming.

SEITAN

Seitan is wheat gluten which is very high in protein. It is available in most health food stores. A favorite in Chinese cooking, it has a meat-like texture which my cats love. I give it to them often. They prefer the type that comes in its own gravy. Sometimes I mix together strips of chicken and strips of seitan; this is a favorite dish.

4
Important Nutritional Supplements

The following foods play an important role in creating and maintaining optimum health for your pet. They also act as appetite stimulants, encouraging the eating of vegetables. Use these supplementary items generously.

KITTY SUPPLEMENT

I make my own homemade mixture that I call Kitty Supplement (KS). I combine lecithin, yeast and *Vegecat*. Sometimes I add spirulina and/or powdered kelp. I use this supplement freely, sprinkling it on vegetables and salad. KS along with fresh raw vegetables will help trigger your cat's digestive enzyme responses. But be patient, it doesn't work overnight. The lecithin emulsifies fatty wastes and boosts the immune system. This will help do away with skin problems like dandruff and dull, dry fur. The nutritional yeast will supply protein and B vitamins. Our systems (cats and humans) can assimilate these vitamins easier when they come directly from a food source like nutritional yeast, rather than from a pill. *Vegecat* is a great supplement. Besides vitamins and minerals, it supplies taurine, an amino acid that cats can't live without.

KITTY SUPPLEMENT (KS)

The basic recipe is:
1 cup nutritional yeast
1/4 cup *Vegecat*
1/4 cup lecithin

You may want to add any or all of these:
2 tablespoons spirulina
1 tablespoon powdered kelp
4 taurine capsules (500 mg. broken open)

Mix all of these ingredients well and store in a tight-lidded glass jar. For convenience put some of the KS in a shaker top container, making it easy to sprinkle on food.

This is something that I have used for years. I have never met a cat who didn't like the basic recipe. The KS mixture is a great way to introduce a cat to new foods like raw or cooked vegetables and grains. Try sprinkling it on sprouts or on a spoonful of green peas.

VEGECAT

James Peden, author of *"Vegetarian Cats and Dogs,"* synthesized non-animal sources of taurine, vitamin A and arachidonic acid. He developed the supplements *Vegecat* and *Vegekit.* (There is also a variety for dogs called *Vegedog*.) The oven-baked recipes he includes with these veterinarian-approved supplements are probably the healthiest way to feed cats a vegan diet at this time. It is my feeling that cats and dogs need fresh food and some of it should always be raw to promote health. For this reason I do not recommend the *Vegecat* recipes as the only food source. *Vegecat* comes with recipes for making your own vegetarian dry 'kibbles.' These products, as well as James Peden's book are available from: Harbingers of a New Age, 717 E. Missoula Ave., Troy, Montana, 59935-9609, telephone: (406) 295-7603 Email: vegepet@aol.com.

NUTRITIONAL YEAST

Make sure that you buy nutritional yeast and not baker's yeast. Flakes are preferred over powder because they are easier to eat dry. I consider yeast a super-food. It is rich in B vitamins, amino acids and minerals. It promotes hair growth and healthy, steady nerves. It strengthens the immune system and helps to repel fleas. If you want to get your cat or dog friend to try something new to eat, sprinkle some yeast on the food. Some cats seem to develop an allergy if fed too much yeast, which is why I recommend 'sprinkles' diluted with other ingredients.

LECITHIN

In addition to emulsifying fatty wastes, lecithin helps to regulate fat assimilation. It brings alertness and steadiness to the nerves, and promotes good skin and hair growth.

SPIRULINA AND CHLORELLA

Spirulina and chlorella are blue-green algae grown in fresh water. They are both high in minerals, vitamins (especially vitamins B-12 and A), amino acids and antioxidants. Blue-green algae are the richest source of protein and chlorophyll. They are very easy to digest. They strengthen the immune system and can protect against cancer and the formation of tumors. A powerful blood purifier, they have been shown to alleviate joint pain due to arthritis.

Spirulina in powdered form is very useful when mixed with grains such as millet, rice and barley. I find the tablet form is just too big for a cat to eat, so I stick to the powdered variety.

Chlorella comes in both a small tablet form and a granulated form. The granulated form is great sprinkled on rice, pasta or vegetables. Chlorella in tablet form is very much liked by my cats. Our preferred brand is *Sun Chlorella* by EarthRise. I usually serve three or four tablets as an after meal treat; they like it so much they would probably eat the whole jar!

A food is generally classified as a builder or a cleanser. Due to their high protein levels the blue-green algae are building foods, but because of the high chlorophyll content they are also cleansing foods. If nutritional yeast is super-food, blue-green algae are miracle-foods.

VITAMIN E

Always buy the natural-source variety of vitamin E capsules, listed as d-alpha tocopheryls, not dl-alpha tocopheryls. Do not buy mixed tocopheryls as they are difficult for cats to digest.

Supplements for a mighty meow.

If your cats have been accustomed to eating commercial cat food, and lots of fish, especially tuna fish, they may be suffering from a deficiency of vitamin E. The high amount of unsaturated fat that these foods contain destroys this necessary vitamin. Cats love the strong smell and taste of tuna and can easily become addicted to it. For this reason it is used as an ingredient in many commercial cat foods. A very low grade of tuna is used, certainly not anything that you would easily recognize as fit for human consumption.

When vitamin E is sufficiently depleted, a condition called steatitis results. A cat suffering from steatitis will at first appear extremely nervous, eventually becoming supersensitive in all the nerve endings in the skin. To pet or even touch a cat that is suffering from this condition is to cause her more pain—the nerve endings are just too sensitive. Giving vitamin E can help to prevent this condition, but only massive injections of vitamin E administered by a veterinarian can cure steatitis. But the most important part of the healing must be to exclude commercial pet foods. Nearly half of the raw material that comes from the rendering plant is unsaturated fat in the form of old restaurant grease. Thanks to the abundance of fast food restaurants these days, there is no shortage of rancid animal fat.

Vitamin E has many benefits. It is helpful for the functioning of a healthy heart, skin and fur. It is also an antioxidant, providing protection against toxins in food and the environment. Vitamin E boosts the immune system. Puncture the capsule (200 or 400 I.U.) with a knife or pin and add directly into food, perhaps mixing it first with a little vegetable oil. Or apply directly to the fur of a forearm which the cat will lick off. Give 200 I.U. twice weekly, or 400 I.U. once a week, for each cat. Be careful that you do not overdose your cat. Vitamin E is not water soluble; it is not excreted in the urine.

TAURINE

Taurine is an amino acid found in meat. Chicken, turkey, tuna, mackerel, clams, oysters and heart are the best sources. The highest levels of taurine are found in raw meat and raw fish. It is hardly found in vegetable, eggs, or milk products.

Dogs seem to do fine on a total vegetarian diet, but cats can become taurine deficient if fed only vegetables. Make sure you supply your cat with enough natural sources of taurine. Their bodies cannot synthesize this amino acid; they must get it from their diet. Taurine deficiencies show up as retinal atrophy which leads to blindness, and liver and heart dysfunction. This serious condition can occur to cats who have been fed exclusively commercial pet food. Because taurine is extremely susceptible to high temperatures it breaks down during the rendering process. For this reason, pet food manufacturers add a taurine supplement to their formulas. Unfortunately, this additive could be destroyed due to the temperatures involved in pet food manufacturing. Even cooking raw meat at home for your pet will destroy up to 80% of this nutrient. If you are feeding your cat fresh food which includes vegetables, grains and cooked meat it would be helpful to supplement the diet with taurine capsules, to be on the safe side.

Since I like to make sure that my cats are getting enough taurine, I add extra capsules of taurine to the Kitty Supplement. It seems to be tasteless and the cats don't seem to notice it, but their health will. Studies show that the daily feline requirement for taurine is 25 to 50 milligrams.

Even though canned tuna, clams and mackerel have undergone cooking in the canning process they still contain high levels of taurine and should be used, but only as an occasional treat. Be cautious of raw meat. Although it is the highest source of natural taurine there is the danger of parasites.

GARLIC

Garlic is on the top of the list as a cancer preventative. It is a good antioxidant and antibiotic. It is also very effective in controlling fleas. Cats and dogs seem to enjoy the taste. I use garlic cloves and powder in cooking meat, eggs, pasta or grain dishes.

SALT

Adding a little ordinary table salt or tamari soy sauce to your cat's diet can encourage her to drink more water. Drinking ample amounts of water can help prevent urinary tract problems and constipation.

OIL

I use only cold-pressed oil. Flaxseed oil and olive are what I serve most. Secondarily I serve safflower, sesame and corn oil. One-half to one teaspoon per day of oil is a good dose.

When cooking for my cats I usually use olive oil or butter. Never cook with flaxseed oil because the heat destroys its health promoting qualities. With the addition of flaxseed oil you will see a noticeable difference in the fur of your pet. This oil promotes a lustrous coat, eliminates bald spots, and assists in the passing of hairballs. Flaxseed oil is a great source for Omega 3 essential fatty acids.

Small amounts of evening primrose oil can be very helpful in correcting dry skin and eczema. Evening primrose oil has been shown to help reduce tumors. These fatty acids are a preventative for cancer.

Wheat germ oil is a great source for vitamin E, although it tastes very bitter and most cats don't like it. Mix the oil in their food or put a little on their fur which they will lick off.

5

Should a Vegetarian Serve Meat to Their Cat and Dog Friends?

The two most difficult questions facing a vegetarian might be: Is it ethical to keep pets, and should those pets be vegetarian also? Over the years I've been urged by my students to write a book outlining my views on cat care. I had been reluctant to write this book. Although I am a vegetarian I endorse the feeding of meat, fish, eggs and dairy. This may seem hypocritical. I suffer a conflict involved with feeding my cats. Being a Yogi practicing ahimsa (non-violence), I am confronted with the question: Do I feed meat to my cats? Is it another form of violence to force my cats to become vegetarians? I wrestle with these questions.

In my opinion the world would be a happier, safer and more peaceful place if everyone (human and non-human alike) were vegetarian. The choice to become a vegetarian should never be forced or imposed by someone else, as this only results in physical and emotional ill-health. But when the mind is rooted in an ethical commitment to vegetarianism the whole body responds in a harmonious way. Intelligence and compassion then direct the actions of a person.

Ahimsa is a *practice* toward perfection, knowing that perfection can never be obtained. We cannot be totally free of causing harm to others as long as we are living beings. Our very presence causes others (if only microbes, small insects, etc.) to be harmed or killed in order to insure our continued life. The ethical practice of non-violence becomes one of trying to cause the *least amount* of violence.

It is a generally held belief that cats need the nutrients in meat, and that it is their preferred food. If the vegetarian in me doesn't like this, I should consider getting a deer or goat for a companion.

My cat Thai Tea prefers vegetables; raw meat on her plate causes her to run away screaming. Sometimes weeks or months may go by before she'll eat the cooked meat on her plate. I make this choice possible for her by offering a wide variety to choose from at every meal.

Most authorities agree that dogs can safely be fed a vegetarian diet. Perhaps cats are capable of becoming total vegetarians too. I choose not to experiment on my cats. I do not advocate a purely vegetarian diet for your cat. There are varying opinions. Ingrid Newkirk, founder and president of PETA, suggests feeding cats a vegetarian diet. The cats of James Peden, creator of Vegecat, are also vegetarian.

Many say that cats cannot be vegetarian. According to Dr. Richard Pitcairn, D.V.M., Ph.D.,

> A diet that excludes meat is not the best for the cat....
> Cats have certain needs that can only be supplied from animal tissues. Unlike both humans and dogs, they cannot convert the beta-carotene found in vegetables to vitamin A....
> They also need a pre-formed source of arachidonic acid and ample levels of taurine, an amino acid not present in plant foods.... We just don't know all there is to know about the nutrients cats normally obtain from meat.

NATURAL HEALTH FOR DOGS & CATS
Richard H. Pitcairn, D.V.M. and Susan H. Pitcairn

Some may criticize me and say that it isn't natural for a cat to eat a carrot. She wouldn't do that in the wild. Neither would a cat attack and eat a German shepherd or a cow (some common ingredients that may be found in commercial pet food), in the wild. Traditionally, since their domestication, cats and dogs have eaten our leftovers; for the most part we have not eaten cats and dogs. Cats and dogs aren't living as wild creatures anymore and neither are humans. Human greed has caused a complete upheaval in the life patterns of all the creatures and plants on this earth. These days it is difficult for a cat to live as a hunter of field mice and birds, just as it is difficult for the Native American to hunt buffalo and to practice the old ways. A cat with a healthy appetite likes vegetables. Just give them a chance. The first things my cats choose to eat on their plates are the raw vegetables.

The following is a list of suggestions that may lead to a more compassionate way of life, minimizing selfishness and greed. Let's start this practice right in our own homes by being kind and thoughtful, and treating the non-human animals who live with us with the respect and the dignity they deserve as fellow inhabitants of this planet.

1. Don't aggravate the situation of overpopulation and animal exploitation by participating in kitten and puppy mills in the form of pet stores and breeders. Instead adopt unwanted animals from your local shelter or humane society. All of my cats have been adopted after being rescued from grim circumstances. Support local spay and neutering programs to reduce the numbers of homeless pets.

2. Feed less meat and more variety to your companion animals. My cats' diet consists of 30% meat; the remaining 70% is from vegetable and grain sources. Many of the meals they are served are vegetarian or vegan. They eat less meat than the 'average pet' and the meat that they do eat is of the highest quality available. It is a challenge to try to offer a noble creature a chance at a happy life when there are so many restrictions placed on their freedom and dignity. Commercial pet food manufacturers claim that their products contain a proportion of meats, grains and vegetables, but I question the quality of these meats, grains and vegetables.

3. Feed only organic, free range meat to your pet. As the dominant species we humans determine the quality of life available for so many creatures. Not only do I struggle as a vegetarian making food choices for my cats, I also wrestle with the apparent contradiction of keeping a 'pet' and practicing ahimsa. To the question: Do I promote the meat industry and the evils of the factory farms and slaughterhouses by feeding my cats meat? I answer: I try not to, by feeding only organically-fed and free range meats, but most importantly by feeding less meat and more organic vegetables. The differences in the quality of the life and the humane methods of slaughter between large factory farms and small organic and free range suppliers are an important consideration.

4. Keep all utensils for handling meat and cooking pans for meat separate from other utensils. If you are a vegetarian you may wish to wash pet dishes separately from other dishes.

WHAT TYPE OF MEAT TO SERVE

I buy organic meat from health food stores. I serve chicken and turkey the most, and very occasionally beef. I serve chicken livers and hearts about once or twice a month, supposedly and hopefully from organically fed and free range chickens. I also serve pre-cooked, sliced turkey and roasted chicken from the health food deli.

Raw meat is the best source of taurine, an essential amino acid that cats cannot be healthy without. Highest sources are found in chicken and turkey. Other sources are heart, tuna, oysters and clams. Heat affects taurine—cooking the meat denatures the amino acid. So the most logical plan would be to feed your cat raw meat. It is the food of choice of cats in the wild. Raw meat has more active enzymes. It definitely has higher levels of taurine, but it may also contain more parasites. For centuries cats have been eating raw meat in the wild with no harmful effects. When the immune system is healthy, a strong digestive system can withstand parasites. But most cats that have been kept as indoor pets with little exercise, and fed processed foods, do not have strong, healthy immune systems. To eliminate the risk of parasite ingestion cook the meat you are feeding to your pets.

Although cooking raw meat destroys about 80% of the taurine, by cooking fresh meat you know your pet is getting some of this essential amino acid from a natural source.

Mamuska's taste for sprouts baffles the experts.

Considering all of this, I do feed my cats raw meat a few times each month.

IMPORTANT PRECAUTIONS WHEN SERVING RAW MEAT:
- Only buy meat which has been labeled organic and is free from added hormones and antibiotics.
- Buy a small amount that can be eaten within two days.
- The meat must be fresh, not frozen and then thawed.
- It must be stored in an airtight container (preferably glass), in the refrigerator.

FISH

Fresh fish is best. My cats like poached trout, flounder, bass and salmon. I also serve shellfish. Raw clams and oysters are a very good source of taurine, but could also harbor parasites. Cooking destroys parasites, but it also destroys most of the taurine. So this is a decision that you have to make, to feed raw or cooked?

I always keep canned salmon, tuna and sardines on hand. When serving canned fish it is healthier to serve with grains such as rice or millet and a lot of vegetables. Canned fish should be an occasional food due to its high ash content and in the case of tuna fish, the risk of vitamin E depletion. Add vitamin E squeezed from a capsule before serving, to counteract this possibility. Even with their drawbacks, these canned foods are still far superior to any commercial 'food' that comes out of a can or box. When storing canned leftovers in the fridge, transfer the contents to a glass container.

DAIRY PRODUCTS
My cats have never been big milk drinkers. It is a myth that milk is the perfect food for cats. Many cats are intolerant of milk. I will only serve milk that comes from organically fed cows and is free of hormones and antibiotics. I serve yogurt about once a week, usually organic goat milk yogurt, and goat cheese once in a while. Parmesan cheese used as a sprinkle on vegetables, grains and pasta I use occasionally. Again buy the organic variety. I do use organic butter occasionally in cooking for the cats.

EGGS
I only buy eggs for the cats which come from chickens who have been fed organic food. My cats prefer their eggs soft boiled or scrambled. One half an egg for each cat is a good serving. They like eggs most when they are scrambled and mixed with rice, seitan or beans and vegetables. (See **CASSEROLE CONVENIENCE MEALS**.)

6

Sample Meals

Some people have reacted to my suggestion of feeding 'human' type food to pets by saying, "I can't afford a fancy food processor!" Most of us have become so blinded that we equate pet food with something that is all mashed up and of a murky brownish color, like the contents of a can of commercial pet food. Before the big pet food manufacturers created their products cats and dogs didn't have their food all smashed together.

My cats prefer eating and savoring one thing at a time. Many cats like the texture of a mashed up meal, probably because they're just used to it. A food processor can be of use if that's the case. Or simply mash and mix with a fork.

The following recipes are all favorites of my cats. Remember that cats are people too and are capable of diverse appetites. The best advice is to be creative and experiment with a variety of foods and combination dinners.

SOME PRACTICAL ADVICE:

- **Be patient.** Don't expect your companion animal to embrace this new diet immediately. Mix it half and half with the old food. Expect to throw out uneaten meals.

- **Serve on an empty stomach.** Remember the 4th Step in the 9 Step Program? Give your cats a chance to change by allowing their appetites to grow in between meals.

- **Don't leave food out for nibbling throughout the day.** This is the first rule in developing a healthy appetite and a strong immune system. If after a half-hour, there is still food remaining in the bowl, throw it out.

- **I feed my cats twice a day.**

The following are some favorite meals enjoyed by my cats. But don't get stuck in a rut. Variety is the best rule to follow.

If you want to serve a meal free of meat it is easy to adjust these recipes. Just substitute seitan and some kind of bean for the meat.

Use Kitty Supplement with added taurine and cold-pressed oil to add zest and nutrition to all these meals.

PERFECTLY LOVABLE LIMAS
Lima beans boiled with hijiki seaweed
Clover sprouts
Kasha
2 steamed green beans
Ground turkey fried in butter or olive oil

KHITCHARI MICE MASH
Khitchari
   (see recipe in CASSEROLE CONVENIENCE MEALS)
Steamed broccoli
2 sardines
Corn off the cob
Mesclun salad

GOTCHA SQUASH
Ground turkey sautéed in butter
Green peas
Steamed kabocha squash
Steamed potatoes

ALL ABOUT TROUT
Poached trout
Brown rice
Lima beans boiled with hijiki seaweed
Clover sprouts
Steamed asparagus

GOBBLE DEE GOAT
Ground turkey sautéed in butter
Clover sprouts
Spirulina Millet
   (see recipe in CASSEROLE CONVENIENCE MEALS)
Goat cheese
Yogurt

Tail-up Tuna, an easy macro meal.

TAIL-UP TUNA
Canned tuna
Arugula
Green peas
Fusilli pasta

TURKEY BLEAT
Sautéed ground turkey in butter
Spirulina Millet
   (see recipe in **CASSEROLE CONVENIENCE MEALS**)
Clover sprouts
Yogurt
Goat cheese
Brown rice

THAI TEA'S CORN DREAM
Corn, steamed and cut off the cob
   (or left on the cob for an exciting chew!)
Steamed kale
Red leaf lettuce
Brown rice
Canned salmon

Bringing in the broccoli kill.

CHICKS 'N BEES
Garbanzo beans (canned)
Spirulina Millet
    (see recipe in **CASSEROLE CONVENIENCE MEALS**)
Sliced turkey
Clover or mixed sprouts

BROCCOLI SWIRL
Canned salmon
Grated raw carrots
Steamed broccoli
Fusilli pasta with olive oil and garlic
Parmesan cheese (soy or dairy)

MAMUSKA MELANGE
1/2 soft boiled egg
Steamed asparagus
Steamed red potatoes

COZY CORNER
Quinoa with scrambled eggs and canned salmon
Winter squash
Clover sprouts
Lettuce

Mezzo Miasma

Eastern Medley
Green peas
Couscous
Cooked de-boned chicken
Finely shredded green leaf lettuce

Crab Prix
Quinoa with crab meat
Hijiki seaweed
Green peas

Mezzo Miasma
Pasta with butter and sautéed garlic
Parmesan cheese (soy or dairy)
Steamed broccoli
Grated carrots
Leaf lettuce
Canned salmon

Floret Mamuska
Steamed broccoli
Grated carrots
1/2 soft boiled egg
Fusilli pasta with grated parmesan cheese

I'm a pea-popper.

CORNY COLLINS
1/2 soft boiled egg
Kale
Green peas
Steamed corn off the cob
Goat milk yogurt

AMBROSIA URSULA
Khitchari
  (see recipe in **CASSEROLE CONVENIENCE MEALS**)
Mesclun salad
Steamed broccoli
2 sardines
Corn off the cob

If you feel that the meals given are too complicated then at least try to follow a simple rule when buying food for your pets: Only buy food that is fit for human consumption.

If you have found yourself unable to prepare a 'home cooked meal,' you can throw together a quick meal by mixing a can of lentil soup and a can of tuna or salmon together. Break open a

500 mg. capsule of taurine and add it. This will make a great meal in a hurry. No need to even cook. Please don't rely on this type of meal for daily dining. In a hurry, on occasion, it can work.

I always keep several cans of soup and organic chicken broth, organic jars of baby food, frozen peas, corn and a few cans of fish (salmon, tuna and sardines) on hand for meals in a hurry.

CASSEROLE CONVENIENCE MEALS

The following meals are easy to prepare and keep well in a tight-fitting container in the refrigerator for several days. They can also be frozen. Be sure to thaw thoroughly before serving. Don't rely on any one of these meals as 100% complete and balanced. In other words, don't feed only one of these meals daily for weeks, months or years. Serve these meals with a raw fresh salad made from finely chopped lettuce, arugula, mesclun, grated carrots or sprouts. Sprinkle with KS or parmesan cheese (soy or dairy), add some flaxseed or olive oil, and toss.

If you are making the transition from feeding your cat commercial pet foods these Casserole Convenience Meals can be helpful. Mix them half and half with the old food. After about 30 minutes throw out everything that wasn't eaten. Never leave food out for nibbling.

The Khitchari and Spirulina Millet recipes provide nourishment and great taste. They serve as a basis for many of the meals.

KHITCHARI
A thick Indian porridge
1 cup brown rice
1 cup red lentils
4 cloves garlic
1 teaspoon salt
5 cups water

Cook over medium heat for 20 minutes. Reduce heat and continue cooking for 40 minutes. Makes enough for many cat meals and one or two human meals too.

Spirulina Millet

1 cup millet
2 cups water
5 tablespoons spirulina powder
5 tablespoons flaxseed oil
1 or 2 tablespoons tamari soy sauce

Bring millet and water to a boil and then reduce heat. Cook for about 20 minutes or until all water is absorbed. Remove from heat. Mixing well with a fork, slowly add spirulina powder and flaxseed oil. Add tamari soy sauce.

You may wish to add one of these to each meal:

Taurine capsule (500 mg.), broken open
Vitamin E capsule (200 I.U.), broken open

Slammin' Salmon

1 cup cooked brown rice
7 1/2 oz. can salmon
1 cup organic frozen corn (thawed)
6 oz. or 1 cup seitan cut into small pieces
4 tablespoons flaxseed oil

Mix all ingredients together well.

Guppy Mash

1 cup Khitchari
6 oz. can sardines packed in water
2 tablespoons flaxseed oil

Mix all ingredients together well.

Turkey Scramble

6 oz. ground turkey
2 organic eggs scrambled
4 cloves finely chopped garlic

Pan fry the above ingredients in 2 tablespoons butter or olive oil. After cooking add:

1/2 cup canned garbanzo beans
3 tablespoons plain yogurt

Mix all ingredients together well.

Miten getting very serious over quinoa.

MITEN'S REQUEST
1 cup cooked quinoa or brown rice
1 cup organic green peas
6 oz. can tuna fish, crab or mackerel packed in water or oil
2 tablespoons KS

Mix all ingredients together well.

URSULA BURST
12 oz. container of seitan
12 oz. can of garbanzo beans
3 scrambled eggs
6 oz. fresh fish
2 tablespoons flaxseed oil

Mix all ingredients together well.

OATMEAL ZEAL
1 cup cooked oatmeal
1/2 cup organic milk or plain yogurt
1 tablespoon flaxseed oil

Mix all ingredients together well.

Kasha Mamuska

KASHA MAMUSKA
2 cups cooked kasha
1/2 package lima beans
1/4 cup pre-soaked hijiki
7 1/2 oz. can salmon
2 tablespoons flaxseed or olive oil

Mix all ingredients together well.

CATS A'LURKIN'
1 lb. ground beef sautéed in olive oil
1 heaping tablespoon of chopped garlic
2 cups cooked quinoa
2 tablespoons finely chopped parsley
1 cup seitan cut into small pieces

Mix all ingredients together well.

SEAWEED SPREE
2 cups Khitchari
2 tablespoons pre-soaked hijiki
2 tablespoons flaxseed oil
1 teaspoon KS

Mix all ingredients together well.

Hmm, only shoe bottoms usually smell this good!

KITTY COUSCOUS
1 cup cooked couscous
1/2 cup toasted wheat germ
12 oz. can lentils (organic if possible)
1 cup seitan finely chopped
1/2 cup cottage cheese
2 tablespoons cold-pressed oil (flaxseed, olive or sesame)
2 tablespoons KS

Mix all ingredients together well. Sprinkle with
parmesan cheese (soy or dairy) before serving.

POLENTA DEMENTA
1/2 cup dry polenta
4 eggs
1/2 cup grated cheese
1/2 cup canned aduki beans
1/2 cup cooked zucchini, finely chopped or grated
2 tablespoons KS

Bring 2 cups of water to a boil and add polenta, stirring with a
fork. Cover and simmer for 10 minutes. While still hot add
eggs and cheese. Mix in zucchini and beans. Allow to cool
before adding KS and taurine or vitamin E.

A lady always has her morning tea.

My cats have large and very versatile appetites. It is a wonderful challenge for me to come up with meals that excite their palates. I am continuously surprised at their willingness to taste something new and outside of the so-called 'cat-norm.'

Ursula, the cat who drinks strong Irish black tea with honey and soy milk with me in the morning, has been doing this since she was a kitten. I didn't encourage her into this civilized habit. She was so insistent, butting her head into my teacup, that I had to pour some into a saucer for her. Now I always make her a small saucer, adding a little extra soy milk, as she likes her tea somewhat milky. We both enjoy our morning tea together; it's a *purr*-fect way to start the day!

7

Poisonous Plants, Flowers and Cleaning Products

A healthy appetite is good, but there are certain things that cats should not eat, even though they may seem to desire them.

There are many plants that are toxic and poisonous to cats and dogs, causing illness and even death. Here are some common dangerous plants and flowers:

Daffodil	Poinsettia	Mistletoe
Philodendron	Holly	Lily of the Valley
Easter Lily	Tiger Lily	Iris
Oleander	Amaryllis	Azalea

The National Animal Poison Control Center (NAPCC) has an extended list of the most common plants, both toxic and non-toxic, including associated problems and hazards. To receive this list write to:

NAPCC
College of Veterinary Medicine
University of Illinois
Urbana, IL 61801

If you suspect your cat has been poisoned contact the NAPCC 1-800-548-2423.

We need to be diligent in providing a safe environment for our cats and dogs. Most household cleaning products are poisonous to cats, dogs and humans. When you wash or wax your floors put your cats in another room until the floor is completely dry. Because of their concentrated ingredients, even environmentally safe products can be dangerous to cats.

It is best not to use fabric softeners on clothes or towels that you are planning to give to your cat or dog. The chemicals are easily transferred to fur, and then licked off and ingested.

8

The Way to a Cat's Heart
is Not Always Through the Stomach

Because I live with cats in a New York City apartment most of the
following suggestions are directed towards cats not dogs. Here are
some suggestions on compassionate pet care for humans who live
with cats:

CLEANLINESS

Before entering your apartment, remove your shoes. Your cats
spend a lot of time walking, sitting and lying on the floor. The
cleaner your floors are the cleaner your cat will be, externally and
internally.

Never touch or pet your cat with dirty hands. The reasoning
behind this should be obvious. Everything that touches a cat's fur
eventually will find its way into the stomach. A good rule to follow
is to minimize the ingestion of toxic and harmful substances. The
result will yield better cat health.

CUTTING NAILS

Never sanction declawing. It is a cruel and barbaric practice.
Declawing is a surgical procedure where not only the claw but
the whole digit is removed. It is comparable to amputating fingers
or toes. It is not only physically abusive but psychologically
hurtful. The cat is left with an impaired sense of balance and a
vulnerability which I believe no amount of tender loving care will
be able to cure completely.

If you were one of the millions of viewers who saw the movie
"*The English Patient,*" and reacted with sympathy towards Willem
Dafoe's character who suffered the agony of having his thumbs

Shall we do a French manicure this time?

amputated, then maybe you can understand what thousands of cats are made to endure.

If you are worried about the cats ruining the drapes or scratching the children, a simple solution is to clip their nails regularly. There are special nail clippers you can buy from a pet store. I use a simple human toenail clipper, holding it sideways as I clip. Be careful not to clip too short or you could hurt your cat. Wait until your cat is relaxed, and sitting calmly on your lap.

> *To extend a claw for clipping, press your index finger on the bottom of her foot while pressing with your thumb just behind the base of the nail on top of the foot. Press gently and the claw will slide from its sheath so that you can get at it with the clippers you are holding in your other hand.*
>
> Natural Health for Dogs & Cats
> Richard H. Pitcairn, D.V.M. and Susan H. Pitcairn

Or you could simply give your cats something to dig their claws into. Something that is their very own. (See **Climbing**.)

Blood supply, do not disturb.

Claw at rest   *Claw extended*

Use a human-type toenail clipper.
Hold steady and cut.

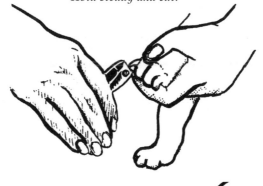

Be careful to only cut the tip.

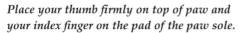

Place your thumb firmly on top of paw and
your index finger on the pad of the paw sole.

Press gently with an upward movement and
the claw will automatically extend.

Illustrations adapted from The New Natural Cat, Anitra Frazier

LITTER BOX

First and foremost the litter box should be kept clean. All waste material should be removed from the litter box twice daily. It is an act of politeness for a cat to cover its excrement. A cat does this for your benefit, and also for the other cats in the household. Failure to cover excrement could be a sign of defiance—they are trying to tell you something. It may be a complaint about the condition of the litter box. Pay attention to these signals.

What kind of litter is best? The best litter is one that is non-toxic to you and your cat. Clay litters with added deodorants are definitely to be avoided. The fine, almost powdered type of clay litter, called 'scoop' or 'clumping litter' can be very dangerous to your cat, and especially to kittens. The dust inhaled from the litter can lead to respiratory problems for humans and cats. Some of the litter can get stuck on the cat's paws and fur, which can be ingested. This is dangerous. Mixing with the fluids in the cat's body, it expands up to 15 times its original size, coating the intestines with a cement-like substance which can cause severe intestinal problems, dehydration, intestinal blockage and even death. But because of its scoopability this type of litter has its advantages. Waste material is easy to isolate and remove. This makes it very attractive to pet owners.

There are many natural alternatives to clay litter. There are good ones made from pine, alfalfa, hemp and corn. I have been using pine pellets with much success. They absorb odor very well and leave no dust or tracking. When the pellets are moistened with urine they turn into sawdust. I also use litter made of corn. The advertising on the bag states that it is edible. I wouldn't go that far. Commercial cat chows make the same claim. Be careful, some cats may eat it. This can cause stomach and intestinal disturbances as it can become lodged in the intestines and cause a blockage.

If your cat is accustomed to only one type of litter, introduce the new type gradually, mixing half and half with the old, and

A cat's eye view of the world (or at least the apartment).

eventually less and less of the old type until there is only 100% safe and non-toxic litter in the litter box.

Climbing

Cats are natural climbers; they like to climb up to a certain height so they can look down upon the world, getting the 'cats-eye-view.' I know of many people who confine their cats to the floor level only, scolding, "No, no, get down!" Some of these cats are confined their whole life to the boundaries of an apartment and are never allowed the exploration of space or the exploration into the world of their own bodies. This is very cruel as it retards emotional and physical development. Exploring the physical range of motion expands the range of motion mentally. This is true for humans as well as non-humans. Cats should always be encouraged to scratch and climb because of the exercise it gives to the body. When a cat stretches to scratch, all the muscles of the legs, shoulders and back are exercised and toned. But a cat who is encouraged to scratch *and climb* exercises all the muscles of the body, and develops self esteem and confidence. A cat who isn't allowed to climb or even to scratch will have flabby undeveloped muscles which leads to poor physical and mental health.

Many people are more concerned about their possessions than for the well-being of the living creature they share a space with. If you are worried about the potential damage to your furniture, give your cat an alternative. Most city cats exist in the confines of an apartment; it is their total universe. We can come and go as we like but they are usually imprisoned.

Supply a scratching post for your cat. Felines appreciate this, especially if it is made from rough and coarse material. Venture to be a little creative. Redecorate your home with branches which have fallen after a storm or were left after pruning trees. Well-placed branches will add an environmental naturalness to your décor. Another thing you can do is to tack up pieces of carpet or rough rope to the molding around doorways.

Our cats are homebound unless we take them out. We have built an enclosed 'cage' which is attached to one of our windows. Inside this 15 foot tall cage are several tree branches arranged in a vertical position. The cats climb up these branches to get to a small, enclosed sun-porch on the roof of our apartment building. Ah! Fresh air, sunlight and a view of the spectacular New York skyline! Coming down is just as much of a physical and mental challenge as going up, so there is always a sense of accomplishment after they have climbed to the top and then down home again.

FRESH AIR OUTINGS

We have halters and leashes for our cats, which we use when we take them outside. Halters are much better than collars; necks are delicate! There is a park a block from our apartment where we take them as often as possible. It is good to get those four paws on solid ground once in a while. They enjoy sampling all the varied smells available. Remember that cats and dogs have a very sophisticated sense of smell. Most humans rely on their sense of

C'mon, lemme go
to the top this time.

PHOTO BY DAVID LIFE

vision to inspire and entertain; cats are stimulated by smells. It is a great cure for the apartment doldrums. Several times a year we rent a car and we all go to the country to spend a few days or a week. I remember the look of wonder when one of our cats, Mr. Mouse, saw his first butterfly. He would never have had that opportunity enclosed in an apartment for his entire life.

If you have never taken your cat out of doors, be patient, go slow. Start by just sitting on your windowsill by the fire escape (make sure your cat is wearing a halter and leash for safety purposes). The next step would be to put her in a cat carrier and go to the park. Don't take her out of the carrier, just let her have a chance to smell and listen and watch. This is enough stimulation at the beginning; your cat will be very happy to return home. After a couple of days, return to the park and take her out of the carrier. But keep close to the carrier. Little by little she will feel safe as her self-confidence grows. Eventually you will be able to walk your cat, or rather she will walk you. It is such a joy to see a housebound pet frolicking through the grass, eyes squinting in the sun, tail held high.

BATHING

I bathe my cats about once a month. I use a mild shampoo that could be used on human babies. If a cat hasn't made friends with water as a little kitten she will most likely be afraid to take a bath. You must be patient and calm. If you are calm there's a better chance that she will be calm. Be careful not to raise your voice. Speak in soothing low tones throughout the bathing experience.

Fill the bathtub with three to four inches of warm water, not too hot or cold. Have a small plastic bucket nearby; use this to pour water over your cat. Never run water while she is in the tub, as it will frighten her. I usually comb my cats while they are wet; this is a great way to get rid of old hair. Make sure you thoroughly rinse off all the shampoo. Immediately wrap in a clean, warm towel and rub vigorously. Make sure that your apartment or house is warm and free of drafts. Never use a blow drier, as it could be very frightening. Be considerate, don't laugh at your wet cat no matter how waif-like and cute or forlorn she may appear to you. Cats always want to look their best and can become very self-conscious when wet.

ALLERGIES

Many people complain of being allergic to cats. They say that it is the dander that causes the allergic reaction. Regular bathing and feeding healthy food are two preventive measures which can improve or even eliminate this allergic reaction. In my opinion, cats fed unhealthy food from kittenhood, descendants of generations of canned food-fed cats, can have very toxic bodies. An irritating film of saliva is spread over the cat's body when she grooms. It is not surprising that a person would have an allergic

I promise I'll never roll in the mud again.

reaction to such a poor, unhealthy creature. The physical body is made of food. To have a healthy body you must eat health-giving food.

FLEAS

Never make an animal wear a flea collar. I feel that these collars could lead to health problems and possible dangers to unborn kittens when worn by pregnant mothers. Would you wear a poisonous collar around your neck to ward off insect pests? Don't force your cat to. Remember they don't have hands and are unable to take the collar off.

When a cat's diet is health-promoting, fleas have a hard time staying around. Regular bathing promotes good hygiene and health. Parasitic infestation (of human and non-human animals) is most likely when regular bathing doesn't occur, and when the immune system is suppressed due to unhealthy eating habits. Bathe your cats regularly and feed them health-giving foods. Nutritional yeast and garlic are proven flea remedies. It seems the ingredients in yeast cause a certain odor to be produced in the skin. Garlic can do the same. The key element is sulfur, causing a reaction which emits hydrogen sulfide on the surface of the skin, making it unappetizing to fleas.

NOISE POLLUTION

I live with a Siamese cat who is very vocal. People ask how I can stand the noise. I have to laugh when I put myself in the place of a cat or dog living with human beings. I try to imagine all the human voice-noise they are compelled to put up with. Human voices blaring out of televisions for hours on end. The cacophony emanating from radios and CD and tape players. The chattering of people talking to each other on the phone or within the same apartment. I compare this with the 'few speeches' my little cat delivers in a day. Wow! I wish she'd talk more. How could I, in all fairness ask her to shut up?

I have visited a wildlife sanctuary and have been around tigers, lions, bears and elephants. One of the most extraordinary observations I came away with was how vocal wild animals are. They are continuously talking: from loud communications meant for the others around them, to simple mutterings to themselves. Through domestication this natural expression has been suppressed. Encouraging vocal expression will boost your cat's self-confidence. Find ways to carry on dialogues. Be careful not to lecture. Give them a chance to get a meow in edgewise. Work on improving and developing good communication skills between you and your companion animals through plenty of eye contact and genuine listening.

LONE CATS

If you are going to control another creature's life to the extent of surgically removing their reproductive organs; confining them to the space of an apartment; choosing what and when they eat; what and who they see, smell, taste and hear; at least give them someone to talk to who speaks their language. No matter how much you love them and how much you think they love you, it is cruel to deprive them of interaction with another being of their own species.

SPAYING AND NEUTERING

It is a hard fact that the world is overpopulated with unwanted dogs and cats. Of course the best solution would be for these animals to be wanted, cared for and loved. That is an ideal situation. Spaying and neutering is a solution to help curb the number of cats and dogs that are killed every day simply because no one wants them; it reduces suffering.

Although spaying and neutering may appear to be an extreme and barbaric solution (removing the sexual reproductive organs of other creatures to make them more acceptable as household pets), I feel it is the most responsible first step solution at this time. It is human ego running wild to allow more puppies and kittens to be born than there are homes for. These unwanted animals are then dumped at the animal shelter where someone else must deal with the problem. Meanwhile they wait patiently in their cages for someone to adopt them before their time runs out, so that new arrivals can take their place.

A better alternative to spaying and neutering might be non-surgical birth control methods. Perhaps there will be more humane developments in the future. But for now, most people find it difficult enough to pay their vet bills. The real difficulty originates not in our pocket books, but in a mind set which says that animals are not worth spending money on.

If you are looking for low cost spaying and neutering, please call your local Humane Society or 1-800-248-7729 for SPAY-USA, which will give referrals in many cities.

9
Trust

Dogs and cats have been domesticated for thousands of years. They trust human beings. There is something very wrong with betraying that trust. As a member of the human species I am deeply regretful of the way we humans have abused our relationships with non-human animals.

It sickens me to see cats and dogs on television commercials, enticed to look eager to eat food that may be very harmful, with tails wagging and lips purring.

Donor animals can be found at some veterinarian clinics and hospitals. This practice, often criticized by humane organizations, violates the rights of cats and dogs. In some cases, donor animals are dogs and cats abandoned by their human caregivers because they were unwilling or unable to pay the medical bills. The veterinarians keep them, using them as blood donors. The trusting animals sit in their cages waiting for their humans to come back for them. How would a human react facing a similar fate, locked in a cell to donate blood without their consent?

Recently an investigation conducted by the Humane Society of the United States (HSUS), Humane Society International (HSI), and Manfred Karremann, an independent German journalist, uncovered some shocking news about domestic dogs and cats being killed for fur. Researchers documented the merciless slaughter of dogs and cats in China, Thailand and the Philippines.

> *The investigators estimate that more than two million dogs*
> *and cats are killed for the fur trade each year.... [It's] a multi-*
> *million dollar international industry. The fur ends up on coats*
> *and products, including 'toy' dogs and cats made with 'real' fur,*
> *sold all over the world.*
> THE ANIMALS AGENDA, Jan/Feb 1999

"I am surprised that it takes something like the use of cats and dogs for their fur to get people upset, when so many other animals are slaughtered for our vanity without a thought," says Sandra DeFeo of the Humane Society of New York.

> *The incentive is simple: dogs and cats are available, plentiful*
> *and profitable.... Investigators report seeing dogs in pathetic*
> *gestures of trust and hope wagging their tails as they were tied,*
> *butchered and skinned, some still conscious as the skinning*
> *began. Undercover videotape shows a German shepherd*
> *blinking his eye as he was being skinned. One of the chief*
> *investigators for HSUS/HSI, Rick Swain, notes that while the*
> *death of any animal is a tragedy, there is something uniquely*
> *unsettling about the commercial slaughter of domestic dogs and*
> *cats. He explained, "Looking at these animals, I couldn't help*
> *thinking about the enormous trust that dogs and cats place in*
> *people. The magnitude of the betrayal of that trust was truly*
> *beyond belief, and all to satisfy a selfish desire for fur products."*
> THE ANIMALS AGENDA, Jan/Feb 1999

Recently a documentary film aired on the Discovery Channel entitled, "*War Dogs.*" It dealt with the thousands of dogs that were trained by the United States Army for service during the Vietnam War. Soldiers who were stationed with these dogs recounted how their lives were saved on many occasions by the bravery and keen senses of these dogs. One soldier said, "If a human soldier had been in the place of any of these dogs he would have been awarded a Metal of Honor for courage and bravery." How did the United States Government reward these dogs for their faithful service? The dogs were viewed by the government as 'equipment.' When the troops pulled out, the dogs were disposed of (euthanized) or abandoned.

We don't have to go to China or Vietnam to witness abuse of domesticated cats and dogs. Every day I see dogs, collared and muzzled on leashes being walked by their owners on the streets of New York City. A very stern command from the human in control, "Sit!" and the poor dogs wanting only to be obedient and good, respond to the command. They sit, placing their exposed genitals on the filthy sidewalk pavement. How many people even think to question this behavior as humiliating or degrading to another being? This incident does not illustrate an animal being mistreated in an overt way but I cite it because of its sheer insidiousness.

There are many dogs and cats who are locked in laboratories, the victims of vivisection. Animals are mistreated in circuses to provide entertainment for humans. This form of abuse is sanctioned by a society that frequents circuses unaware of the training methods employed. If we truly wish to live in a peaceful world we must become peaceful ourselves.

10
Yoga Teachings on Non-Violence

In Patanjali's "*Yoga Sutras,*" ahimsa (the practice of non-violence) is the first step towards the attainment of Yoga, which means everlasting happiness. The opposite of ahimsa in Sanskrit is *himsa,* which means harming. Himsa is classified into three divisions:

1. *Physical, by body and instruments, including war*
2. *Vocal, by speaking against others, including psychological warfare*
3. *Mental, by thinking against others*

> *One cannot injure others without first injuring oneself because injury is the result of psychological planning. Vocal injury is more serious than physical, and mental injury is the most serious. By physical injury one can destroy only physical forms. By vocal injury one can destroy both physical and mental forms. By mental injury one can destroy even the form of spirit.*
> THE TEXTBOOK OF YOGA PSYCHOLOGY, Ramamurti S. Mishra, M.D.

Reflect for a moment on the incredible amount of effort and money that goes into propaganda during wartime, to get one side to hate and despise the other. This type of mental injury goes on all the time; it is what fuels racism and speciesism. Degrading and injurious words are in our everyday language. How many times have you heard someone insult another person by calling them the name of an animal? This kind of subtle suggestion fills our minds with harmful and injurious thoughts, and manifests in abuse of animals. We have the mistaken notion in our minds that animals are less than us and do not deserve the right to be left unharmed or unused. Their abuse is easily sanctioned. We live in the effects of our thoughts.

11
Teachings of Love
and Kindness from Dog People

The first time I visited India I was horrified to see the suffering of the many homeless dogs trying to stay alive on the streets in many of the cities and towns. When I looked closer I learned some very important lessons. I am a cat person. Before going to India I had assumed many truths about the behavior of dogs. Some examples: They do not develop family units. The male dog never takes responsibility for the care of his wife or children. When the going gets tough it's "look out for number one" in the dog world. Dogs never drink tea. I will relate to you now a couple of inspiring stories from India which may broaden your perspective on the exceptional capacity of a dog's heart and mind.

MR. AND MRS. DOG AND BABY DOG

We were visiting the ancient and holy city of Benares. On a street near our hotel I would often see a very small, white, three-legged female dog. She always seemed to be in a hurry, constantly on the lookout for any bit of discarded food, on the alert to dodge kicks. When she did find food, she never ate it on the spot, but quickly ran away with her prize. One morning as I was walking down the busy narrow street I heard the whimper of a puppy. I looked under a rotting wooden board, which was being used as a stoop placed over the open sewer drain, and saw a tiny white puppy crouching on the side of the gutter. I didn't really have more than a two second look when a white 'blur' sped in front of me, and to the side of the little waif-like puppy. It was the three-legged female dog. Now that I knew that she was a mommy I regularly bought food for her and her baby. But trying to find their living quarters was a challenge. She often changed homes for security reasons. Sometimes I would be wandering around for hours with a bag of chapatis or a clay cup of yogurt or dal, looking for her.

Sitting on the banks of the River Ganga with a full bag of chapatis feeding a small troop of dogs I became very intrigued with the behavior of one dog in particular. He was quite polite and didn't push or shove his way to the front of the pack, but waited patiently on the sidelines. I sought him out and gave him a whole chapati, which he took and then let drop to the ground between his front paws. He looked up at me imploringly. I was confused. Didn't he like chapatis? But the dog didn't walk away and leave the bread; instead he remained stationed, looking up at me. So I gave him another chapati. He then dropped it on top of the first one, and deftly scooped both of them up in his mouth. He quickly turned away and began to run. I was determined to follow him, and went running down the narrow streets, dodging cows, people and other dogs. I was able to keep him in sight. Then I stopped when he stopped. He ducked his head beneath an old gutter board under a sari shop. Yes, there they were; three-legged mommy and little baby, his hungry little family. To look into their grateful eyes and see their wagging tails, you could tell that they were all very happy. Dad had brought home the bread today, and how! The valiant Little Daddy, as I called him, stood guard in front of the gutter while his wife and child ate their chapati dinner. When someone tells me that dogs are incapable of strong family ties, I have to shake my head and say, "You just don't know what you're talking about."

CHAI FOR THE DOG

While in Benares, we were invited to breakfast with the family who owned and ran the hotel we were staying at. We arrived at their living quarters, several rooms on the ground floor of the hotel. As we were waiting for breakfast to be served we became acquainted with the family's pet dog, a little, white fuzzy Pomeranian named Julie. The wife of the family inquired if we had taken our morning tea yet. We admitted we had not and said that we would love some. In a few minutes she returned with three teacups filled with golden steamy fragrant chai. She gave us each a cup and put the third cup on the floor for Julie, who sniffed it and decided it was much too hot. She patiently sat down behind her cup and waited until it cooled. When a few minutes had passed, Julie delicately began to lap up her tea with her long, pink tongue, pausing every few moments to look up, making eye contact as if to say, "Oh my, this is a superb cup of tea, isn't it?"

APPRECIATION

When staying in India I am always on the lookout for hungry dogs. I carry food to give to them, and got into the habit of never leaving my hotel room without being 'armed' with provisions for any dog I might run into. I came to know several regulars. There was a very sick and skinny female dog whom I had started to feed every afternoon. She was covered in mange and was in very bad shape. Before she would eat the food that I brought to her she would always pause and look up into my eyes as if to say, 'Thank you.' She never grabbed the food and ran off with it, she never started to eat before showing her appreciation with that look in her eyes. After a few days she began showing up to meet me around the same time, at the same spot on the street. My friend David became very concerned. He was worried that I was making her dependent and when it came time for us to leave India in a couple of months, she would be without any charitable human friend and this would be very disappointing to her. Wasn't I concerned about that? Of course I was, but I also knew without a doubt that what I was doing was best. I tried to explain it from the following point of view.

Remember now, we are in India, where the generally held belief is that wherever you find yourself in this life is the result of

God is Dog; Dog is God. Dogs all over India happily await Sharon's karma yoga.

your past actions, your karma. If someone, anyone, human or animal, finds himself in an unfortunate situation, it is because they performed bad actions in a previous birth and are trying to redeem themselves in the present birth. Some people feel that sick and starving dogs on the streets are receiving just punishment for their previous karmas and that we should not interfere. If you are born a dog then you must have done horrible things in your past life. In many cases the attitude is to increase the pain and suffering by inflicting more pain and suffering. It is common practice in India to beat, kick or throw stones at dogs, simply because they are dogs. I've come to see that if we hold on to anger, resentment and hate, our hearts will have little room for love, forgiveness and compassion. If someone has performed horrible crimes in past lifetimes which has resulted in their present birth as a dog, what will stop the cycle? If that dog's only experience of humans is fear, anger, resentment and hate, what hope does she have of liberating herself from more and more miserable lifetimes? As long as she holds these negative emotions in her heart she is bound. If we can show that dog some unconditional love, a moment of kindness that can allow her heart to feel appreciation or forgiveness or gratitude instead of fear and anger, her soul is that much closer to rebirth in a better situation. I am willing to do what I can to help that process along. Love and kindness are never wasted; they are valid solutions in all situations.

It didn't matter that we had to leave her one day. Everyone leaves everyone some day. What is important is the quality of time spent with another being on any one day.

12

Education

This little book is a beginning. You need to supplement your learning from as many sources as possible. I highly recommend the following books, magazines and videos. They have been written and made by courageous human beings who dared to care. I am forever grateful to the painstaking efforts of the following authors, editors and producers and for the remarkable educational and enlightening material they have given to us all.

RECOMMENDED READING
NONFICTION BOOKS

- *Diet for a New America*, John Robbins, 1998, HJ Kramer Inc, PO Box 1082, Tiburon, CA 94920

- *Food Pets Die For*, Ann N. Martin, 1997, New Sage Press, PO Box 607, Troutdale, OR 97060-0607

- *Natural Health for Dogs & Cats*, Richard H. Pitcairn, D.V.M. & Susan H. Pitcairn, Rodale Press, Emmaus, PA, 1995

- *Vegetarian Cats and Dogs*, James A. Peden, Harbingers of a New Age, 717 Missoula Ave., Troy, MT 59935-9609, (406) 295-7603, vegepet@aol.com

- *Rationale for Animal Nutrition*, Dr. R.L. Wysong, 1998, Inquiry Press, 1880 Northeastman Rd., Midland, MI 48642-7779

- *Keep Your Pet Healthy the Natural Way*, Pat Lazarus, 1986, Keats Publishing Inc., 27 Pine St., Box 876, New Canaan, CT 06840

- *The New Natural Cat*, Anitra Frazier with Norma Eckroate, Plume, New York, 1990
- *The Dreaded Comparison*, Marjorie Spiegel, Mirror Books, New York, 1996
- *You Can Save the Animals*, Ingrid Newkirk, 1999, Prima Publishing, PO Box 1260BK, Rocklin, CA 95677
- *250 Things You Can do to Make Your Cat Adore You*, Ingrid Newkirk, Simon & Schuster, New York, 1998
- *Ranch of Dreams*, Cleveland Amory, Penguin Books, New York, 1997
- *The Cat Who Came for Christmas*, Cleveland Amory, Penguin Books, New York, 1995
- *The Textbook of Yoga Psychology*, Ramamurti S. Mishra M.D. (Shri Brahmananda Sarasvati), 1997, Baba Bhagavandas Publication Trust, 13 Sapphire Road, Monroe, New York, 10950
- *Louis Wain—King of the Cat Artists*, Heather Latimer, Papyrus Publishers, New York, 1982
- *The Cat Inside*, William S. Burroughs, Viking Press, New York, 1992
- *Peaceful Kingdom Random Acts of Kindness by Animals*, Stephanie Laland, Conari Press, Berkeley, CA, 1997
- *Healing With Whole Foods*, Paul Pitchford, North Atlantic Books, Berkeley, CA, 1993

FICTION BOOKS
- *Particularly Cats... and Rufus*, Doris Lessing, Alfred A. Knopf, New York,
- *Old Possum's Book of Practical Cats*, T.S. Eliot, Harcourt Brace & Co., New York, 1982
- *The Fur Person*, May Sarton, W.W. Norton & Company, New York, 1983

MAGAZINES

- *The Animals' Agenda*, Kim Stallwood, editor-in-chief, 1301 S. Baylis St., Suite 325, PO Box 25881, Baltimore, MD, 21224, www.animalsagenda.org

- *Earth Island Journal*, Gar Smith, editor-in-chief, 300 Broadway, #28, San Francisco, CA 94133, www.earthisland.org

- *Animal Times*, Ingrid Newkirk, editor, PETA, 501 Front St., Norfolk, VA 23510, www.peta-online.org

- *Best Friends Magazine*, Michael Mountain, editor, Best Friends Animal Sanctuary, Kanan, UT 84741-5001, www.bestfriends.org

- *Nexus Magazine*, Duncan M. Roads, editor, PO Box 30, Mapleton Qld 4560 Australia, www.peg.apc.org/-nexus

VIDEOS

- *The Animals Film,* directed and produced by Victor Schonfield and Myriam Alaux, 1987, SlickPics Int., Inc., MPI Home Video, Oak Forest, IL, 60452

- *Diet for a New America,* produced by EarthSave, Fox Lorber Associates, 419 Park Ave., New York, NY 10018

- *A Cow at my Table,* directed by Jennifer Abbott, produced by Flying Eye Productions, 1998, Denman Place Postal Outlet, PO Box 47053, Vancouver, BC, Canada, V6G 3E1

- *Henry [Spira]: One Man's Way,* directed by John Swindells, produced by Peter Singer, 1997, Bull Frog Films, (800) 543-3764

ANIMAL RIGHTS ORGANIZATIONS

Please support the following financially or with volunteering your time:

THE HUMANE SOCIETY OF NEW YORK
306 East 59th Street
New York, NY 10022
(212) 752-4842

DORIS DAY ANIMAL LEAGUE
227 Massachusetts Ave. NE, Suite 100
Washington, D.C. 20002
(202) 546-1761

EARTHSAVE
706 Frederick Street
Santa Cruz, CA 95062
(408) 423-4069

FUND FOR ANIMALS
200 West 57th Street
New York, NY 10019
(212) 246-2096

PEOPLE FOR THE ETHICAL TREATMENT OF ANIMALS
PETA
501 Front Street
Norfolk, VA 23510
(757) 622-PETA

PERFORMING ANIMAL WELFARE SOCIETY
PAWS
PO Box 849
Galt, CA 95632
(209) 745-PAWS

BEST FRIENDS ANIMAL SANCTUARY
5001 Angel Canyon Drive
Kanab, UT 84741-5001
(435) 644-2001

Afterward

Animal abuse can come in many forms. To physically, mentally and spiritually chain a dog or confine a cat, forcing him to just sit and watch and wait for his entire life, is abusive. He is physically bound, but he is chained on more subtle levels, too. Bound by subtle thought waves that tell him that he is an inferior being. His mind and heart for generations back has been programmed by the degrading thought that human consciousness is the highest.

Each one of us should examine our own behavior to find ways in which we may be contributing to the suffering of another. We should examine those attitudes that result in harm; those attitudes that we are unaware of because they are condoned by society. Like feeding our companion animals and never looking into what they are really eating.

Perhaps this book will encourage a few people to become more aware. As a result they may stop feeding their pets commercial pet food.

Perhaps legislation will be passed prohibiting the use of pets as ingredients in their own food. But does that really get to the root of the problem? Even if pet food manufacturers were compelled to leave out dead cats and dogs, what are we left with? I feel it is the duty of the consumer to demand the highest quality food for their pets.

Thousands of animals are unwanted and are euthanized every day. A total shift in consciousness is required so that human beings start to treat other animals with respect and consideration, as valued inhabitants of this planet.

Compassionate education is essential for this change of mind. It is our duty to educate ourselves. As we think, so the world becomes.

Strive to see yourself in others, all others, so that 'otherness' disappears and there is only love.

Jesus said, *"Do unto others as you would have them do unto you."* He didn't specify what kind of others. He didn't say: Do unto others as you would have them do unto you as long as they are of the same gender, color, nationality, religion and species as you.

> *A long, long time ago the rocks*
> > *thought they were people.*
> *A long, long time ago the trees and plants*
> > *thought they were people.*
> *A long, long time ago the fish and whales*
> > *thought they were people.*
> *And one day they will be saying*
> > *a long, long, time ago the humans*
> > > *thought they were people.*

Beaver Chief
LUMMI TRIBE, Pacific NW Coast

THIS IS NOT

THE END

IT IS THE BEGINNING

.